Otolith

Otolith

EMILY NILSEN

icehouse poetry
an imprint of Goose Lane Editions

Edited by Karen Solie.
Cover and page design by Julie Scriver.
Cover image: *Boba Fett, the Driven*, copyright © 2015 by Ilja Herb, www.iljaherb.com.
Printed in Canada.
10 9 8 7 6 5 4 3 2 1

Library and Archives Canada Cataloguing in Publication

Nilsen, Emily, author
   Otolith / Emily Nilsen.

Poems.
Issued in print and electronic formats.
ISBN 978-0-86492-962-4 (paperback).--ISBN 978-0-86492-952-5 (epub).--ISBN 978-0-86492-953-2 (mobi)

   I. Title.

PS8627.I55O86 2017   C811'.6   C2016-907041-7
                                             C2016-907042-5

We acknowledge the generous support of the Government of Canada, the Canada Council for the Arts, and the Government of New Brunswick.

Goose Lane Editions
500 Beaverbrook Court, Suite 330
Fredericton, New Brunswick
CANADA E3B 5X4
www.gooselane.com

For my parents,
and their parents.

Contents

Meanwhile

Fog

Fog

Pre-dawn Walk

Who walks
behind you, wringing
your shadow over the marsh?
First frost and beneath the bridge
water slows into ice whorls.
An otter chews through
a trout, chews the gnawing
winter, thins the world around you.
Who skulks through the valley, trapping
your sleep in invisible snares?
                    You step nearer
the river as morning mist lifts
the drowned night
onto shore.

In the Forest I Found an Organ

My amateur forensics
reckon it was dumped last spring.

Recent rain lends it the sheen
of a displaced liver, fresh out

not yet belonging to the moss
it sits on. I distrust spring: the showy

promises. Some things just end.
We keel over from abundance

of hope. Lifelong deflation,
withering like a balloon spiralling

from the sky. I prefer a fall-time forest
when the aspen thin, their heart-shaped leaves

in smithereens. The brittle
keep us honest. Spring forward—

fall back. Today I wear a tool belt
from which dangle a small frying pan

and two rabbit pelts. Over my shoulder
the city scuttles like crabs under a rock, blindly

tinkering ahead.   I approach the organ
with caution, inflate the bellows, to play

a minor chord. It wheezes off-key.
Eight dozen nights outside, sponging up

fog, would do that to anyone. This is the sound
I, too, will make one day.

Directions to Crabapples
Rogers, Scott. Personal Communication.

Keep Baxter Shoal left as you pass
Pym Rocks. Head north
across the east entrance of Fife Sound
and northward up Raleigh Passage, between
the Burdwoods and Pearse Peninsula
of Broughton Island. Hook a left at Trivett
westbound up Penphrase Passage.
Pass Sir Edmund Bay
on your left. Turn northwards
towards Shawl Bay then through
the nameless tight passage
into Moore Bay—
don't run into Thief Rocks.
Continue northwards up Kingcome Inlet
and head NNW where the Inlet diverges
into Wakeman Sound between Upton Point
and Philadelphia Point. Continue northwards

to the Wakeman estuary:

Ha-xwa-mis
Alalco.

Float House b. 1919

I heard cupboard doors open
and close. A trap snapped

without a mouse. I saw a pack
of cannery workers, huddled at the table eating

pork and beans out of the tin.   Didn't I?
Did I?   Sorted postage and stamped letters

in my sleep.

Sewed a new pinafore, one wrote.
Waiting out the long winter, one replied.

　　　Have you seen the ghost? Billy asks.

Fog

Eight-headed fog, plate rattling
fog, dirt under the nails fog, fog
of unseen trees where the blind
follow creeks, fog fattened
by memory, flip-sided fog
and swimming on land fog,
throat-bellied fog of the broken
hearted, night fog that slipknots
three moons to the dock
and knee-buckling fog with spittle
on its chin, fog rotting in the cupboards
and a shelf of pickled fog in jars, shaking
your limbs as you sleep fog, that curls tails
of foxes and wets moth wings to
uselessness, clique forming fog
of kitchen gossip, and thirsty for rain
fog that taps us instead, fog of the floating
house, unknown to undersea fog, fish milt
fog, slap-in-the-face fog, fog that smells
of a logger's boot, untying its apron fog,
rhododendron fog, thick as algae bloom
fog, a pond of bulging frog eyes fog,
that drops poems in your lap and sinks
pebbles in your pocket, thick as gravy
fog, fog to grow old in, bearded
fog, running its hand through
a patch of thinning hair fog,
bacon fat fog, arteriosclerosis
fog, fog staggering half-cut
along the rocks, bottom of the bottle
fog, hooked to the disappearing
dragnet, fog adrift, a bundle
of yellowed love letters washed
ashore, waiting
to be read.

Float House

She holds the damp like a duck down pillow.
Damp as a waterlogged fir. Buckets she hauls in

ache when spilled (sound of oars)
seawater wets my shivering feet.

I mop up sorrow with a dry-wood fire
and wait for the berries to shrivel

before trying again. This house contains both
land and sea, its floorboards tickled

by stickleback and herring, chirp of an otter
beneath the bed. Now, all gone to grass.

Have you seen the ghost? Billy asks.

A Geologist Conducts an Aerial Survey of the
British Columbia Coastline, 1995

While flying at 200 feet he found a large number
of simple curving rock walls along the low tide line of
more than 350 beaches in a concentrated area.

Tide lowers, he circles back.
The sanded underside overturns, lets out
a gull-like mew. At forest edge, a woman
scrapes a bear hide, clouded fat gathers.
Her eyes are set deeper than the sound
of pebbles dropped down a well.

Can we measure
the depth?

We cannot.

Float House

In the bunkroom a presence catches,
quick whiff of propane, a metallic tinge
hits the roof of your nose. Watch the window —
hummingbirds land midair. Spook
the black bears. Ring the gut hammer.

    Have you seen the ghost? Billy asks.

Float House

Night mice. Their nibbling a distraction
from sleeplessness. If mice live on average

two years, these are 48th generation,
a moving insulation keeping the building

upright. Great- and great-great-grandparents
are nocturnal. My eyelids both open and closed,

it's that dark. Latin for *little mouse* also means
muscle. Another translation for *musculus*

is *mussel*. A mischief of mice, their eyes,
all pupil, wink like wetted shells.

    Have you seen the ghost? Billy asks.

And What of the Fog?

Caligo nebula. An extinct species of marine bird
used fog to navigate. Even their tongues were white.
They built nests in the mist and laid round eggs that bobbed
above tree-tops. Without fog, these birds were grounded. Their feathers
useless. Protruding like miniature telescopes their eyes, the colour of clotted
cream, swung towards magnetic north. The thicker the fog, the more certain
the direction. This function made them susceptible to capture by those lost
at sea. The last mating pair poached in 1904 by two fishermen, presumed dead,
while only fifty metres from shore.

And What of the Fog?

It arrives with evening
rainfall like an eclipse
of hungry moths.

Sleep well amidst its patter
on the windowpanes.

And What of the Fog?

No use laying traps.
It will find a way in
and out.

And What of the Fog?

It brings amnesia, blind spots.
Recognize this offering.

Cabin Fever

Every Monday and Thursday, we rush to the dock to receive news of joy
and disaster. Gossip rides on the pulsing back of an eel, enriches the village
like vitamin C. We fend off scurvy and make-believe our way
out of another tragedy. Told or not, stories bubble and fall
between low fog and high tide, pressurized, carbonated
in the indefinite weather, without a boat to board.
People have stopped using language.
Every sound from our mouths
the shape of a different sorrow.

Otolith

Ear Stone. Annuli within vestibule.
Age concentric, dark-light, dark-light,
each season encased in the next.
The centre deep-sea
bottomless, compressed,
an undiscovered pit of felled
        shadows, detached long ago
from their source, stain
of beginning where fish became.

In Order to Say It Exists We Must

measure the distance
between xiphoid process
and brain, seal in Ziplocs
and send to a lab in Kentucky
then subtract or divide it from
itself. We must stalk it stealthily
on our keen kitty haunches, and smell
its odour, pungent, an unopened jar
of beaver castor. In order to say it exists
we must collect its hair, clip its fin, wing,
earlobe, capture it with our cameras, record
the audio, pixelate and play it forwards, backwards,
stack it amidst layers of deep house to play
at a harvest potluck for an upbeat woodsy feel.
We braid it into our own hair, drop it into a bucket
of saline and stare for hours recording
each movement on a spreadsheet.
We give it names like Honeysuckle,
Walter or Specimen A. Item B. Plot C.
Hold its greasy fish-oiled fur in our hands
and indicate in our Rite in the Rain notebook
that it screamed like a mountain lion
when the sun rose.

Meanwhile

Meanwhile, You and I in the Endless

Sun. Grass not yet ripe.
How unbundled we are
in never-ending light. No hatches
to batten. No blue hour
to tuck into. Two
sheets, pinned
   on a line, fluttering
        dry
over the untied
        hayfields.

Meanwhile, Earl Grey in Port Hardy

No fresh-cut flowers
this time of year, just fistfuls
of salal. Sure, let's sit

outside in the puddles
of afternoon leftovers. Inhaling
second-hand smoke from strangers

is one way to feel not so
alone. You pour a thick stream

of canned milk into my BC Ferries mug
and the weight anchors the cup
to my lap. Rain

peels carnations off
the can's dog-eared label.
In the motel parking lot

      we float apart

         on plastic chairs.

Meanwhile, I Take a Glass of Scotch to Bed

because my grandfather, the man who knows
things we may never, wet himself

at the dinner table. Someone, please tell him
he is older than most of us will ever be.

We pad him in a life vest, draw straws
to decide who will push, then look the other way

as he heads out into the bouncing sea.
It is not easy to watch the dying

set adrift, harder yet to know
we are responsible. Some of us cope

by calculating the onset
of extinctions, the sea turned

equation as we seine bucketfuls
of salmon, sea lice sucker-punched

to scales. Copepod. Motile. Chalimus.
Parasitic. The parameters of data

keep hands steady as we skim over
the single-pane of low tide. Below us,

laissez-faire sea cucumbers softly tide-tumbled,
cream anemones in a flop-top thicket, magenta

starfish colonizing the bladderwrack
bedrock, a dimpled surface of young pinks

on their outward migration. And us,
stagnant as a slick of boat oil

lollygagging over slack tide. The water
will decide where we go.

At the Surprise Birthday Party

I try on a baby. Someone across the room
yells, *Hey! Looks good on you!* They are a drunk
rambunctious bunch tonight. I try on
two babies, one on each arm. *Bottle me*, I say

with a pretend slur. Someone sticks a rubber nipple
in baby one's mouth. A dirty blonde with a true bowl cut
talks financials and wealth management at me. I tell her
I have no money to put anywhere, not even under

the sofa cushions, am not yet tired of being broke.
Thing is, she says, *these things are kind of an investment too.*
Koochie koochie koo. She wiggles a finger, the baby
wants to bite it. *Bite it, baby,* I whisper. *Sic'm.*

The moms are in the kitchen rolling joints
on the laminate floor, tight as a pack of hyenas
laughing on the edge of town. So I smuggle
their babies out to the quiet plains flickering:

green — yellow — green —
our secret show.

Welcome…

say the northern lights,
pretending to be neon.

Meanwhile, in His Dreams

My grandfather swims through the arteries
of a blue whale. He heard its 400-pound heart

beating a mile away. I encourage my inconsequence
by choosing the longest checkout line in Safeway,

surrounded by expired discounts, twenty-eight types
of gum, and not one of those magazines

can explain where the whales breed.
We hide grief in secret pockets

of our trench coats. Magic!
It emerges like a bunch of gladiolas,

hops away a red-eyed rabbit.

My grandfather knew sleight of hand,
a glass of water disappearing

beneath his hat. Ten past midnight
he phones to ask where we have left him —

the sea, pale as a desert.

Meanwhile, I Have Started to Fold Things

A beet-stained dinner napkin.
The aluminum lining of chocolate bars.
Unwanted receipts. And sometimes
a square of two-ply as I sit
on the toilet looking at the mole
over my kneecap, a wonky planet
mooned by freckles, my zebra-print skirt
far away on the floor, washed up
against ankles. Nothing fancy,
no origami cranes or ninja
stars: just squares. While waiting
to board the Greyhound I shared my umbrella
with a one-legged boy who told me
a 1 mm thick
piece of paper folded in half
100 times is thicker
than the observable diameter
of the universe,
and would ascend
133,989,789,471
light years away.

My Lip Sits in a Petri Dish, Meanwhile

a city is being nailed onto the plains.
I hadn't noticed that quiet hammering,

the drill-drill-drilling of plywood taming shadows
to shade. It grows faster than a camp

of refugees. Well, says the city as it hangs
a hard hat over itself, the topography

makes it easy. Last night, it fit
under a garter snake, under the thumb

pad of a vole, really
it was just a scratch

in the silt, a friendly-like *psssssst!*
how-de-do? Now it's lumbering

whole, a droopy-eyed klutz falling
drunk into the gold, wind-whispered

foothills only fireflies and coyotes
called home. The light out there

is reckless. It's eaten too many
blue whales and neon dinosaurs, cranky

hearts spin in a centrifuge, bloodshot
from over-sugaring. On a high-

rise patio tiny critters cloister and cauliflower
overgrows in clumped canopies, bursting out

a rooftop pot, my god—
all I see are lips, lips, perfect lips,

overripe unpicked strawberry
mouths, everywhere. They are

everywhere.

Intertidal

Pre-dawn Walk

In the season of creaking rivers
I am kept awake.

Pre-dawn Walk

Past the hardware store
and the on-sale hibachi. Past
the cat curled up in the used
bookstore window. Past the chain-link
fence draped in dried-up hops and past
a garden of rotting squash. Past the woman
who thinks she is Edith Piaf and past the brick
building outlined in ivy. Past the mannequin clad
in fishnet stockings and past the barbershop pole
and a floor of unswept hair.   To the lake, I walk
down to the lake.   Past the bakery
with its lights on and past
the hockey rink with its lights
off. Past the truck idling outside the diner
and past a raven pecking tatty crusts
from a brown bag.   This is the past: the lake
was a river.   I walk over pebbles
towards where sturgeon swim, caught
in their solitary, rugged routes.

Fragile Morning of the Landlady

She shovels the first snowfall
into five even piles. Hinging at the hips,
bending to sidewalk, her terrycloth robe
belted to keep
her heart in.   Yesterday,
she raked a mulch of maple
over the curb. In a divisive November
the electric orange of street lamps keeps us
contained. Her bleak determination.
My silent immobility.

The argument long lost. She sits on the deck,
stubbornly slicing apples into crescent moons
with a dull pocket knife.

Fragile Morning of the Farmhand Who Longs to Leave

The cows surrounded her as she pushed
to the middle of the field through knee-deep snow,
tin bucket on her arm. Between the legs of cattle
and an oak she watched ocean shuffling stiff slabs
of water. Her neck craned to see it: a fishing boat
splitting the sea down its middle. Milk froth.

Fragile Evenings of the Man in His Trawler

Slumped at the table nook
that is kitchen, living and dining room,
he unbuttons his jeans and winces pulling
suspenders from his shoulders. *Northwest Passage* clicks
off, and as he leans to flip the well-worn cassette
notices three piles of sawdust on the floor.

He remembers this detail while writing
a letter he will never send to his daughter.

How good it felt
to hold one hand in the other, bound
only to the boat, its gentle lullaby,
and the clink of mugs in sync with rain.

Fragile Night of the Hitchhiker from Up Island

Cougar full of deer
lugs a sagging second set
of lung, heart, liver up the slide path —

Pow!
            Gunshot ripples the sea. He lowers
the rifle butt from his shoulder notch, leans
against the boat's plywood windshield, '70s hull
rotted like his back molar. Everything with a tender patch,
a fibreglass warble. Even the hard edge mildews. Smack the land, the land

smacks back. *Driving that train, high on cocaine,* whistling to keep busy
through the goddamn rain. Jean jacket soaked in trouble. No woman
to lean over. He can still smell her neck, hot in the sun.
Now he's close, all up in his own face. He went out
like that, fast and loud —
            with a bang.

Fragile Hour of Dementia

The man at the dock paints sailboats
the colour of a cloudless day reflected off seawater.
His back is bare, sun-chewed sinew. He is made of copper
coins and flecked in blue. He hides sculpins in the froth of his beard
and once outswam a pirate off the Polynesian Islands.
Listen, he walks, callused heels
sliverless in a hum of
      la-laa la-laa la-laa

An Address to Dusk

He takes me to the creek
and as he whittles a fallen cottonwood branch,
I wash his shirt. He heads into the forest
and drapes the shirt over his back.
        Still heavy with water
        it drips like a dark fish
        into the soil.

I leave you and follow.

An Address to Dusk

You are behind me
in the kitchen as I pack a suitcase full
of wares: wooden spoons, knives wrapped
in newspaper, a cast iron, the threadbare
dishcloth from Bulgaria.

At the sink, turning
on the tap, I catch his reflection
in the window. And through him, you:

an overturned canoe, lake simmering under
evening sun, a pile of half-stacked wood
bitten yellow with wolf lichen, laundry
hanging limply on the line.

An Address to Dusk

Alone in the alpine meadow
beneath a ridge. Moon rises bent
like the rib of a deer. Stars begin

to peck at the sky, cleaning
and drying bones
of the day.

Screef

By noon I had opened the ground a thousand times.
Fast terrain. Trenches. Shovel-

split the earth no wider than a pack of smokes.
Pine after pine slid in.

Boot stomp. Close the hole. Move on. Easy.
I'm singing—*hell*

yeah—I'm singing. Sun through
cloud cover leading my limbs

as we two-step over slash piles.
Black-capped chickadees call out

from a dog-haired stand of spruce:
Cheeese-burger! Cheeese-burger!

Fastened to my ears like a pair
of garnet clip-ons.

Every camp has a legend.

Breakfast, over scrambled eggs:
Did you hear? That old guy shot a bison.
Butchered strips dry over a snag.
Stink of death pushed up our noses.
Bears loiter, ping-pinging off
the electric fence. He was ancient: *at least forty.*
Kept to himself. A ruddy-faced Czech.   —There he is
traipsing through thicket, shouldering
the muscle of dusk in his backlit mane
of briny hair. Tree-burl calves.
                        Humpback.

Kid, I was born brave.
Never had an apron to hide under.

I am not yet my older self. Everything is
intact, enclosed by spaciousness: I wash my face

in a trough of muddy water and sleep blindfolded
to fend off evening sun. I learn how to shotgun

beer and smoke when angry, bluff-charging
the future. I try on other animal hides

for size. My lungs, pink as a wolf
tongue, strong as a set of moose antlers

mounted to my spine. My skin not yet
chapped to rawhide nor baggy

as the cook's muck-brown lab
and her wobbling sea of lipomas. But—

in certain light, maybe, maybe I notice

airborne pesticides. The list
of brands we inhale grows longer
than my arm. Fungicides, insect-
icides, herbicides. Clusters of alveoli
tweak out, a bad case of witch's broom.

Hooked on antihistamines. Neck high
in fireweed. Wasps scramble out of land-mined
stumps with a low cello drone to protect
the busted city. *You'll hear 'em*
before you see 'em. Keep your shovel in the ground
and for godssake stay still. Fat lips. Swollen eyelids.
Run—
to the marsh. Bites puckered
in swamp water. *Piss on 'em. Cover yourself*
in pennies. Under the glint of copper
my buck-naked heart jolts
upright, twitching.

There are stories underfoot:
balled-up, overturned, now pricked
by caulk boots as we stuff a forest
into the ground. Here in the once timbered
shade, three wolves circled a wobbling fawn
and a fleet of moosehide canoes glided
breathlessly by the oxbow...

Bundles of fifteen, swaddled
in Saran Wrap: spring-tipped, greener
than youth. Mudslide. Cattle. Snow.
Fire will eventually take these trees.

Hot days in the bush get to your head.
Price-per-tree calculations mix with thoughts
of last night's salty mashed potatoes, an empty
rum bottle in the ditch and one drunk-ass
faller-buncher. My brain's on epinephrine
and Kelvin from the Ivory Coast swats deer flies
with a scythe of grass. I'll drink any lake
under the table and scare bucks out the creek
with my dirty shins. Bushed. Hotheaded
blood back-eddies into a semi-stagnant
drip-drip-drip (as we bend
                              then rise
                  then bend) on slow drill. Pacing
to be let out.   We just have to—

Storm on the griddle.
Clouds pinwheel, horizon
forked by lightning. Lick-pop
of a fast fire.

As for the hundreds
of undug holes that will one day
need filling, I can almost hear them:
their pitch, taut as tinnitus, aching
out of an open field, gaping like
un-mothered mouths thirsty for rain.

You are at the junction
where ground wasps nestled
in low-lying stumps and the mountain ash
dropped its berries, caking the floor with orange

and red. Now the forest is all jaw. Charred
moss on logs. You walk through what was once
an aspen grove and snag your sleeve on a black branch.
Cotton rips. You walk on. When your boots scuff

the ground, soot billows, sticks to the sweat
on your cheeks. Your teeth and tongue dried
with ash. The earth still warm with smouldering roots.
You kneel in search of pine cones, seed pods, the crest

of a bulb, something that promises life. Your hands,
thickened by work, feel nothing. The wind finally
reaches you. It runs through the vacant canopy
and then between the buttons and thread

of your shirt. It carries the call of an owl
pulling night forward. The ripped cloth
on your elbow is a pine white butterfly,
lifting as you turn to leave.

Meanwhile

On Day Eight We Cross the Arctic Circle

We appear on the other side scrubbed clean
by wind. It is an imaginary line, a coin pulled
from my ear, earth's receding hairline, a cough

on the windowpane, a seasonal fen that hopes
to replenish itself, hardened yet marshy underfoot,
an ache and an itch. It kills birds in the morning

then brings them back to life. It's the vocal cord
of caribou. Tied to its own demise. It has no texture
but that which it crosses. Walking backwards

will not undo what has been done.

Midnight Sun

The mother wanders the hallway
uncertain of time. She hides

in her nightgown. How pale her cheeks
since her stepson drowned at sea

two weeks ago. A jug of sheep milk
sloshes side to side on the table.

Her family drank 4 L a day.
The ship caught fire, there were

no survivors. In the kitchen
she told me. I looked at my hands,

they were far away on my lap,
and my lap was at the bottom

of a cliff, and the cliff was covered
in white roses, and the roses were falling

all over us.

Yesterday I was paid to scythe
the field. I tried to slice the day

in two. My work shirt and jeans stiff
as plywood in the unbroken gale

that blows evening into morning. At 5 a.m.
the farmer washes his car, buckets water

over the black hood under a V
of honking geese. His black dog

barking. Night keeps its distance
from the farm, cooling the pith

of caves, gnawing winter fleas
from its hind leg.

The village arrives in whispers.
Heads bowed, through the door.

The mother is frying cod in butter.
We ate five hundred kilograms of meat every year.

She speaks to keep death away.
Lamb and fish. Smoked dark

lamb, boiled fish. Darkness,
the smoke. The village fumbles

for wool blankets thick enough
to snuff out the bright, layers

them over windows. Stuffs
door frames. I never met the boy.

In the kitchen's muffled light
four shapes feel around for cutlery

and plates. I cradle a stack
of blankets, a foreigner who

can't find the word
for goodnight.

Little Stick Man with a Knife

Traplines are not lines,
but tracts of land bordered by ridges
and valleys, stitched together by river.

Harold sits at his living room table, crust of age
in the corners of his mouth. Coiled on a cabinet
of fine china, a cougar, shiny-eyed and stiller

than wood. Teacups rattle as Harold crosses
the broadloom. He walks like a mudslide,
pulls out a pile of papers, crayon lines

still bright as lipstick. His mother made him
trap muskrat in the ditch. Harold Age Eight
drew them strung on the fence and him,

little stick man with a knife. Using his palm
as a map, he traces the route, half a century walking
his own animal trail, in, out the pines, the light

of winter closing over his back. In the garage,
the animals droop on hooks. Silt-free rivers
tint beaver fur blue and there, stretched

on a hoop, the pelt: round, glaucous,
tight as life. At eighty, Harold prods
at his past, close enough to touch

its underbelly fur,
with a fear so fresh
it walks without ribs.

Mouth of a River in Greenland

My nephew takes a break
from beachcombing to place
a frilled oyster shell over his ear.
Hears the groan of an iceberg, sighs
of narwhal tusks twisting as they grow.
Under a mile of ice, a hidden canyon winds
740 km to the Arctic Ocean. At three and a half
my nephew's bones are beginning to sigh too.
We move driftwood and the imprints fill
with water. In thirty years he will be thirty-three
and a half and the mouth of a river in Greenland
will have its tongue pulled out, pinned to the news.
A smashed geode, hush-hush words spat out to sea.
NASA research shows there is still a lot left to discover.
Multichannel Coherent Radar Depth Sounders
penetrate layers of ice and measure bedrock
below. Landscape-level X-rays uncover a new
Grand Canyon to ride our donkeys down.
Today my nephew likes dinosaurs, superheroes,
pink runners and visits to the aquarium
where we peer up at a plastic narwhal
as it sways from a row
of fluorescent lights.

Meanwhile, I Wait for You in Arrivals

Coated in the dust of post-winter
country roads. Sad snow piles, seeping grit,
leafless trees splattered in paper cups, hillsides

hide ground with a beige grass comb-over.
Since you left, the snow has melted salt stains
onto my trouser hem. On the airport TV

an Albertan rancher is crying about flooded land,
where to put his cows. This town is full of women
with popped-out veins. Muscular as elk, they could

squash me between their thighs. They eat
grass, have babies, drink kombucha, have more
babies, and the creeks keep rising. I wait

with a styrofoam cup of Husky tea
between my knees. Last week I met a man
named Malcolm who builds stone circles

in the forest. He told me how thirty winters ago
a freak storm blew snow over his plastic windows
in the Arctic. For weeks everything was dark,

and they had to eat leather. You disembark.
Passengers herd forward. We have learned
to live like the river we live on: in one direction,

with preprogrammed dams opening
then shutting their concrete gills. Water
obeys, our lives are in order.

In the Cornfield with a Horse

It is dark, you lie in a clearing.
The horse is beside you, to be safe.

Last night you climbed into the bathtub
wearing long johns, listening to the rabbit

in the moon. *Run*, it said. Hiding
was not an option. Your body

had become a machete, sharpened
on stone, turning on you. Life

is mean. The orangutan's hands
were cut off when she ran too slow, or

not soon enough, a child once
on her back, now she lies

under a kilo
of ant-eaten leaves.

Meanwhile

My grandfather fiddles with his IV
and I count one hundred and sixteen

saline droplets. His body so happily
estuarine, no longer landlocked.

In Vancouver, creeks once ran
their brackish mouths, seagulls

dropped clams, the thwacking
city streets blockaded by fireworks

The celebratory do not know
how to meet our eyes. I admire

the doctor's Converse, unapologetically
upbeat on the mint floor. She describes

a clear plastic phone from the '80s,
multicoloured wires visible — *no*

she is referring to my grandfather, who
once said, even if the pretty yellow flowers

along the highway are considered noxious,
never stop appreciating the vista, cynicism

won't lead to happiness. Empathize
with viruses, like most of us, they fight

to survive. With my right foot I nudged
the porpoise off the shore to which it kept

returning. Despite trying, I cannot tolerate
inane inventions (sleeping bags

for cats, star-shaped ice trays, slippers
with flashlight toes). Invent a vacuum

to suction Piscine reovirus
from the Pacific and Atlantic.

The doctor removes
her stethoscope to ask

What virus? What sea?

Fog

Return to the Coast

Hello squinting thrash of sea,
you wriggling baby. I would hold you

if you'd let me. Hello kidney bender,
bulging disc and misplaced memory,

there you are. Choppy slate, dirty tooth
grind crossing. Old lumpy, you've churned up

the humpbacks. One and two,
three and four pluming herring,

deep sigh —
Deep six

the years, the already dead, my dog
bitten calf, and heck, our dying lung.

The sink is full of dishes
no one wants to clean.

Hello shipwreck leaking diesel,
eight life vests bobbing. I am down

with the ship, a captain
so parched my muscles fused

to bone. My sea, hello.
I ran from you.
          I rain for you.

And What of the Fog?

Before a storm, its stench
was as though a wet mammoth
had shaken itself at the door.

And What of the Fog?

Pan-pan, pan-pan. An elderly man in a rowboat
has been lost for twelve days. *Seas 1 to 2 metres building
to 2 to 3 late this afternoon.* Creaking rowlocks
curdle your dreams. *Fog implies visibility less than half a mile.*
His cotton ball eyes. His temporary cataracts.

And What of the Fog?

For nine days we were tangled
in it, during which time we lost
the use of the letter O.

And What of the Fog?

If pushed in by a southeast wind,
it will carry the smell of flowers.
Birds-of-paradise in December,
winter rose in July.

And What of the Fog?

Be kind. It only wants
to be held.

Burdwood Islands, Ten Years Later

Mostly the same.
Though I can hardly remember
what it felt like to sleep on the beach
beside you. We had both forgotten
our toothbrushes and that night it rained
the scent of wild mint. To get to the island
we took turns rowing, facing each other,
legs in legs, one backward, the other
forward. Revisiting the beach now,
I crunch over crushed clams, dried urchins,
a jerry can ditched in the bush, and want
to know exactly when and why
the cedars dropped their branches.
The tree we camped under is no longer
a tree. It is gaunt. Sun-beaten yellow,
soon to be twisted like the others
that jut out from rockshore. I am writing
to retrieve that forgotten part of us,
the part we left behind.

Every rock I overturn
is rimmed in dried-up
rings of brine.

Directions to the ~~Burdwoods Fish Farm~~*
Rogers, Scott. Personal Communication.

From the ~~Midsummer Island fish farm~~, cross ~~Spring Pass~~
towards ~~Retreat Passage~~ and leave ~~Green Rock~~ on your port side,
before heading to the entrance of ~~Retreat Pass~~ and the waters

between ~~Bonwick Island~~ and ~~Gilford Island~~. Head north
into ~~Retreat~~ between ~~Success Point~~ and ~~Seabreeze Island~~.
You will see Gwa-yas-dums and their big house.

As you pass the ~~Fox Group~~ on your port, the ~~Upper Retreat fish farm~~
will be starboard. Head into ~~Cramer Pass~~ and go east towards
~~Echo Bay~~. Once past ~~Evan Point~~ on ~~Baker~~, veer north past ~~Echo Bay~~

then continue north mid-channel towards the ~~Burdwoods~~, keeping
~~Pym Rocks~~ on your port and ~~Powell Point~~ on your starboard.
Head towards the western edge past ~~Village Point~~ on ~~Denham Island~~.

The ~~Burdwoods fish farm~~ is anchored
to the island, located in the protection
                                    of this bay.

* Where ~~text~~ = Musgamagw Dzawaḏa'enux̱w Traditional Territory

Otolith

The pressure to return was mutual.
Chum to river, river to chum. It seemed

watertight, even if a tad unruly. By spring freshet,
the salmon's egg had grown fins, fed glacial runoff

through its scales, and from the river, an imprint
stored behind its brain. Every year a new ring.

In labs under microscopes, scalpels splice fish skulls,
tweezers pluck out hyaline buttons, lasers sniff out

geography, chemical combustion, mini-museums
of aquatic travel: an island inside a lake on an island

in the ocean, our solar system, diagram
of the universe, a ripple, parallel

occurrences, sound waves, withered
eye of an elephant, dendrochronology,

a volcano's perfectly mapped topography.
The otolith core is wrapped in opaque sheets,

time and space deposited
by nutrients. Yet, upon magnification,

the lines are not defined. *Shhhh,*
shhh, shhh — hemlock needles drop

in soft trillions, the chum,
their final nitrogen push.

Meanwhile, the Anchorage

They come in yachts
to buy bags of iceberg lettuce
from the marina. Squish-squash
down the dock in honeymoon
deck shoes. I row out, fetch
the crab trap, bailing the rowboat
with my rubber boot. *Boss. Prosperity.*
Ocean Dollar. Damsel. Darling. This evening
we share a patch of undulating sea. We piss in it
then warm ourselves with dinner as dusk
closes in. *Glorious.* The dabbling rain,
cashmere cardigans. A tooth-marked cob
of corn bobs past my oar, then a handful
of embers barely aglow, washed out
by the unseasonal tide. Anchors adrift.
Daddy-O. Fat Chance. Farewell, I pull away —
delaminated raincoat stuck
like unborn skin to my back.

And What of the Fog?

It wants us to stay.

Notes and Acknowledgements

Italics from "A Geologist Conducts an Aerial Survey of the British Columbia Coastline, 1995" have been lifted from the trailer for the 2005 documentary *Ancient Sea Gardens*. The italics from "Fragile Night of the Hitchhiker from Up Island" are from the Grateful Dead song "Casey Jones."

"Casey Jones" Words by Robert Hunter. Music by Jerry Garcia. Copyright © 1970 ICE NINE PUBLISHING CO., INC. Copyright Renewed. All Rights Administered by UNIVERSAL MUSIC CORP. All Rights Reserved. Used by Permission. *Reprinted by Permission of Hal Leonard LLC.*

Earlier versions of several poems have appeared in *PRISM international* and *Lake*.

Thank you to my parents, Wendy and Carl Nilsen, for their unwavering support and for passing on the gene that enjoys long stretches of alone time. To my aunt Angela, for showing me how to make art a priority. To Pegge Marshall, for always asking for more words. To Liz, Meg, Finn, Esme, Emilia and Leif, for being blood and bringing love.

Thank you to Scott Rogers, whose friendship and knowledge of the Broughton Archipelago I have come to rely on. To Yvonne and Al, for inviting me to pick raspberries and stretch my sea legs when cabin fever set in. To Billy, for feeding me plates of deep-fried fish and for using the word "kidney bender" in reference to the rough boat ride we were about to take. To Nikki, for offering up a cabin when quiet was needed. Thank you to the Salmon Coast Field Station, for always agreeing to shelter me in a place where my bones feel aligned. The field station is located in Kwikwasut'inuxw Haxwa'mis territory, thank you to the surrounding forests that carry this light.

Thank you to Trudi Smith, for hauling me into the backcountry with tent-shaped camera obscuras and offering bottomless inspiration. To Eileen Delehanty Pearkes, for always appearing at the right time. To Sheryda Warrener, for bridging past and present lives. To Sonnet L'Abbé, for conversations and reading recommendations that sparked a number of poems. To Melanie Siebert, for knowing what matters.

I gratefully acknowledge the financial support provided by the Social Sciences and Humanities Research Council, and the Faculty of Creative and Critical Studies at UBC Okanagan for the Graduate Research Award and Graduate Fellowship Prize. Thank you also to Nancy Holmes, for generosity, wisdom and willingness to converse with multiple mountain passes in the way. To Sharon Thesen, Michael V. Smith and Matt Rader, for providing input and advice. Thank you to the Woodhaven Eco Culture Centre.

Thank you to Karen Solie, for leaning into the poems with your editorial intuition and general brilliance.

Thank you to Kari Michel, for your curiosity and love of the unknown, it keeps us skipping.

To everyone at Goose Lane Editions and icehouse poetry, thank you for guiding me along.

photo: Kari Medig

Emily Nilsen was born and raised in Vancouver.
She has published poems in *PRISM international*, *Lake*, and
the *Goose*, and in a chapbook entitled *Place, No Manual*.
Nilsen was a finalist for the CBC Poetry Prize in 2015,
after having been longlisted for the prize on three separate
occasions. Her work has also been longlisted for the
UK National Poetry Prize.
She lives in Nelson, British Columbia.